Inspiring Expressions!

How to Draw Activity Book

ActiviBooks for Kids

1
2
3
4
5
6

1
2
3
4
5
6

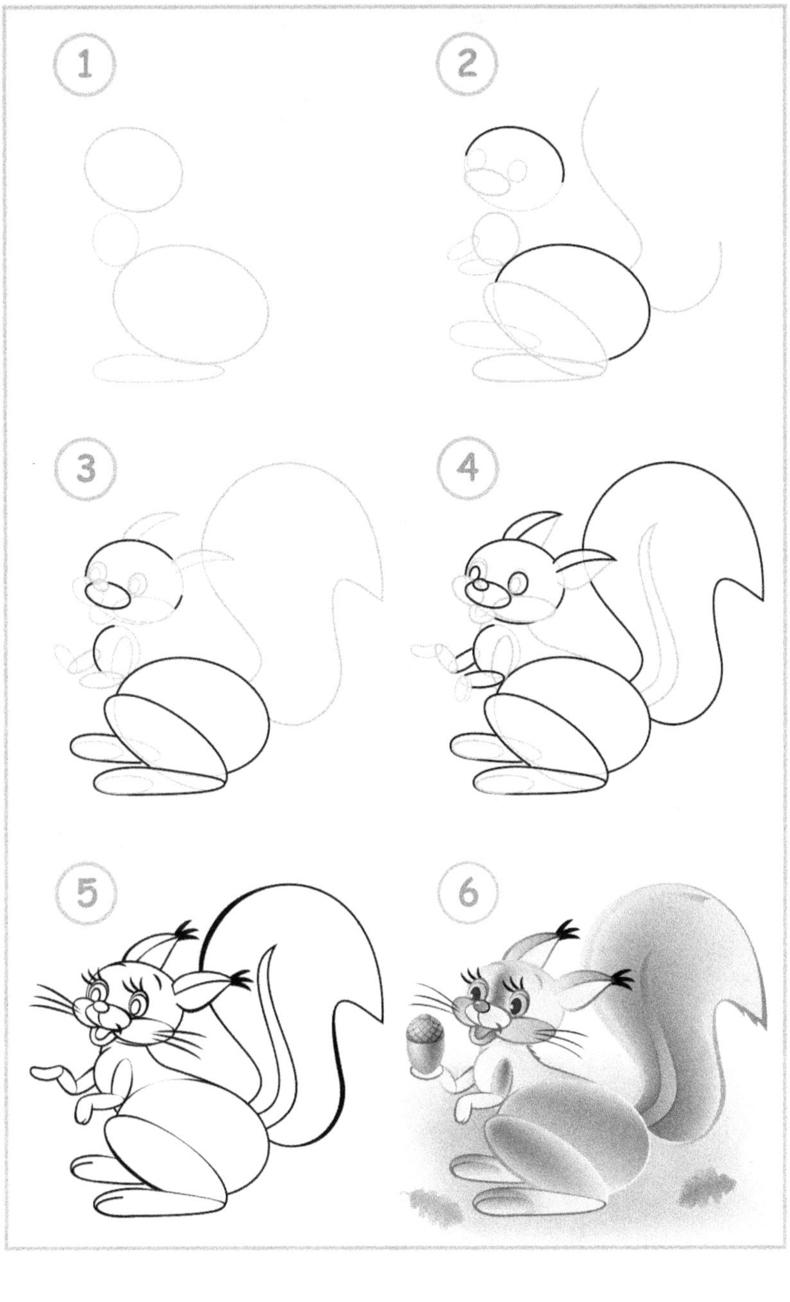
1
2
3
4
5
6

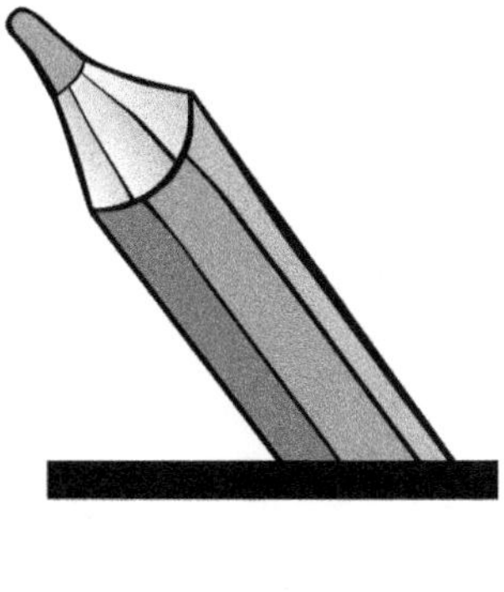

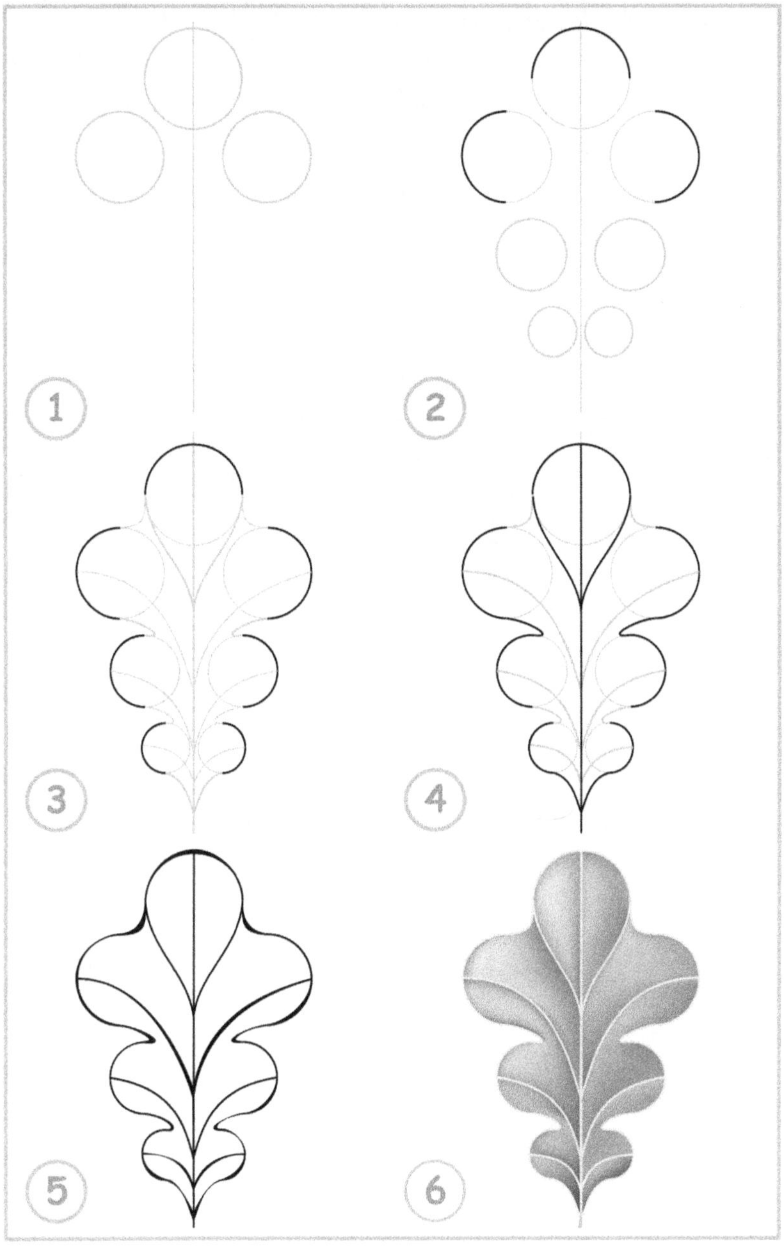
1
2
3
4
5
6

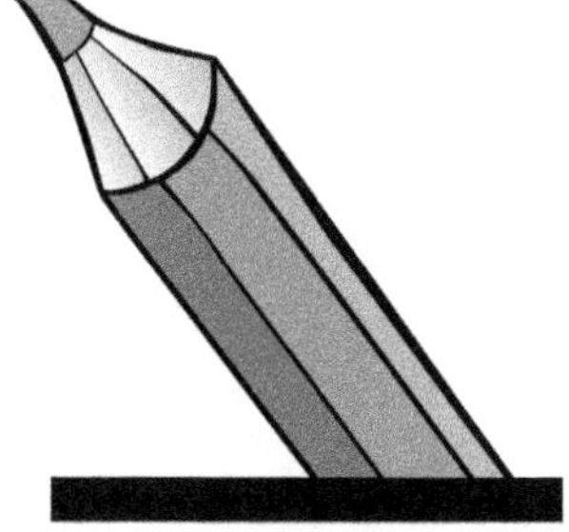

1
2
3
4
5
6

1
2
3
4
5
6

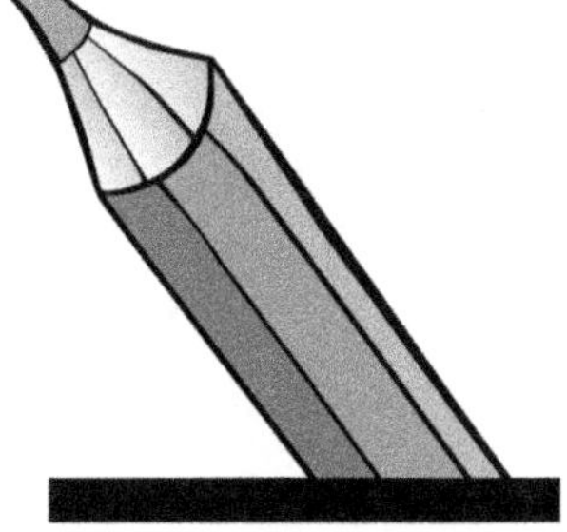

1
2
3
4
5
6

1
2
3
4
5
6

1
2
3
4
5
6

1
2
3
4
5
6

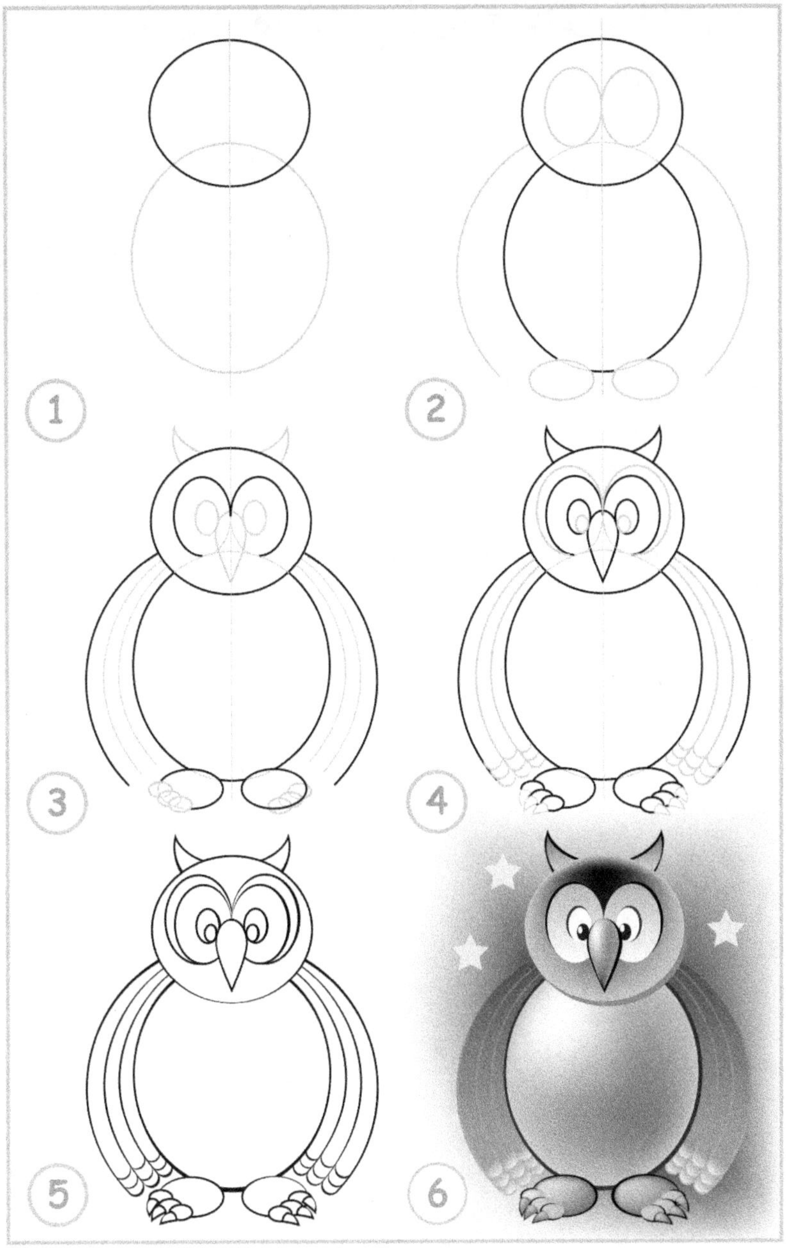
1
2
3
4
5
6

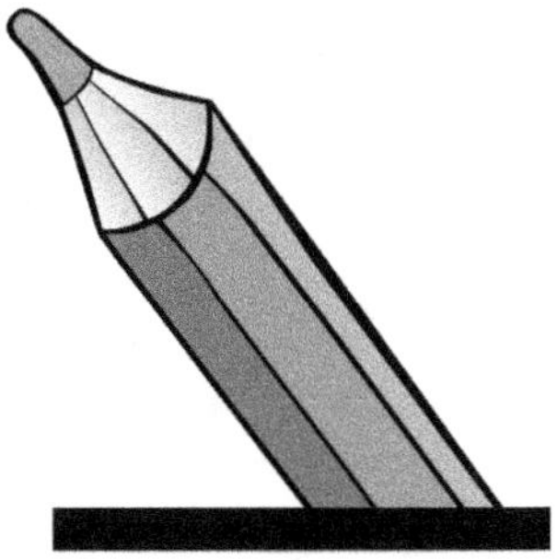

1
2
3
4
5
6

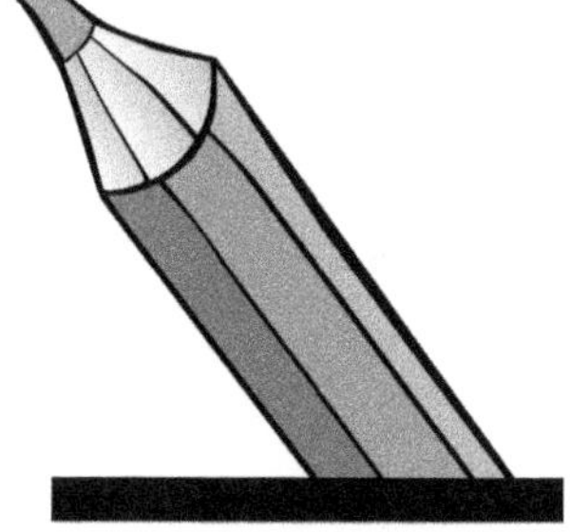

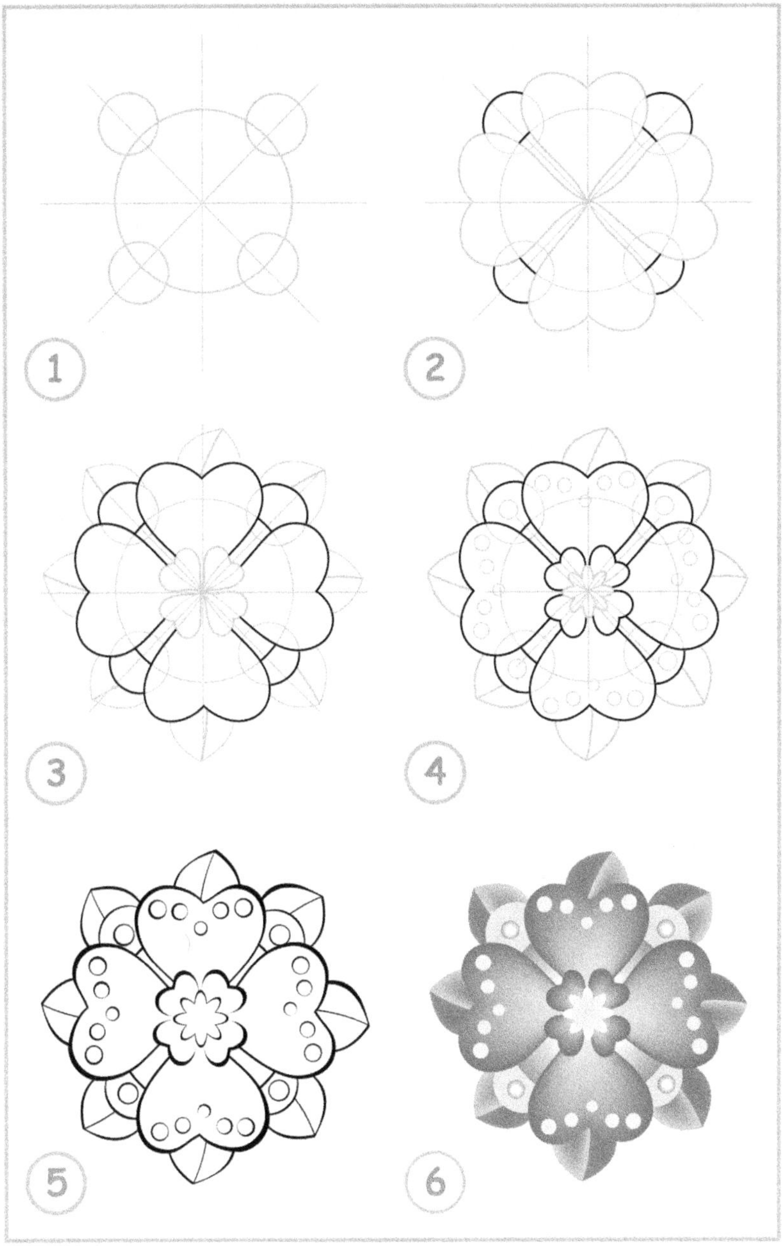
1
2
3
4
5
6

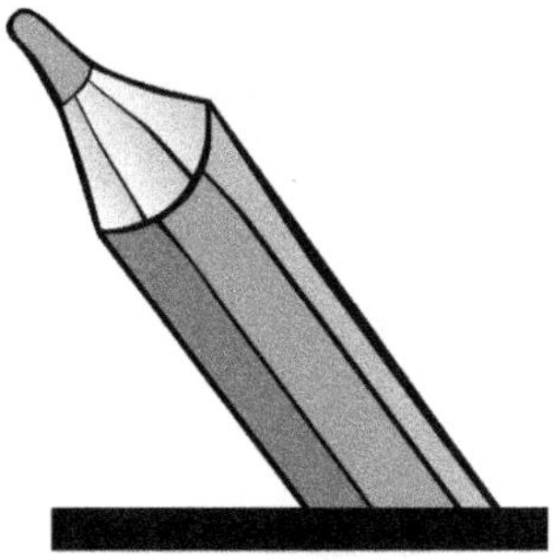

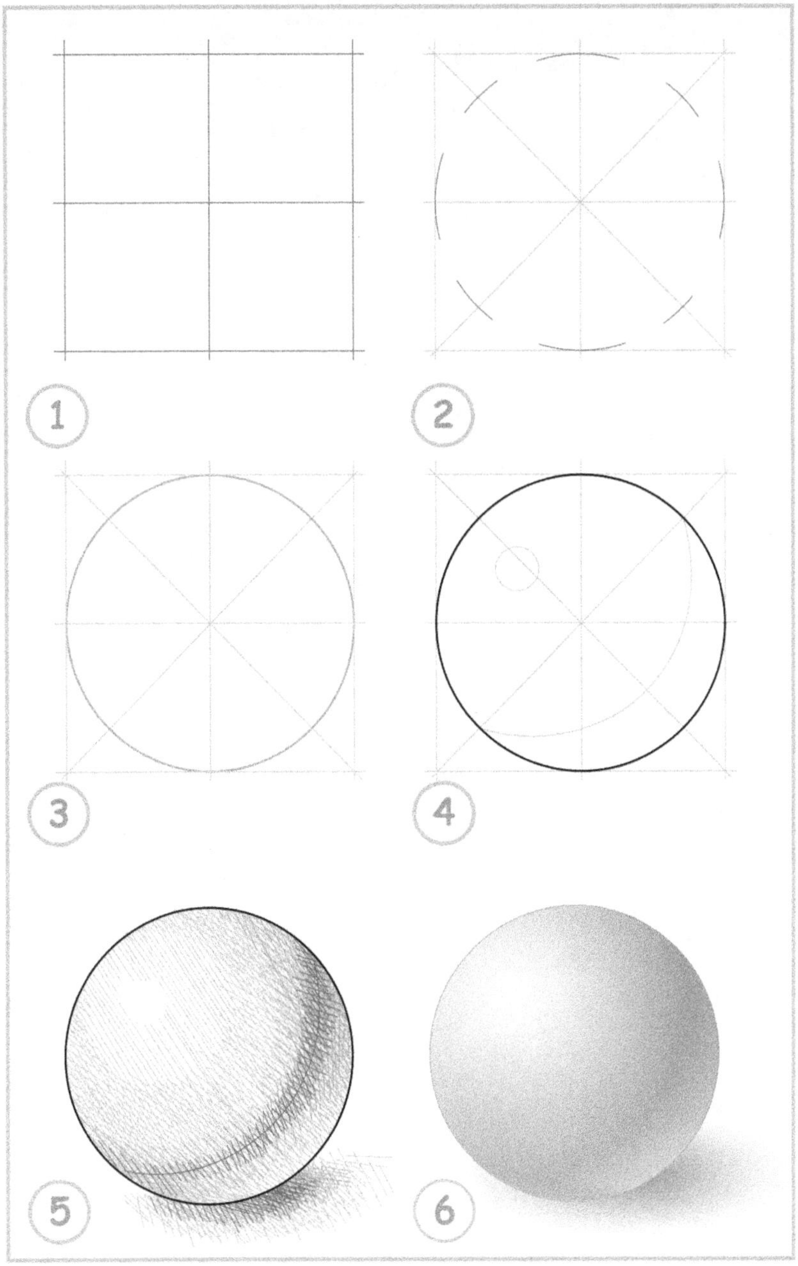
1
2
3
4
5
6

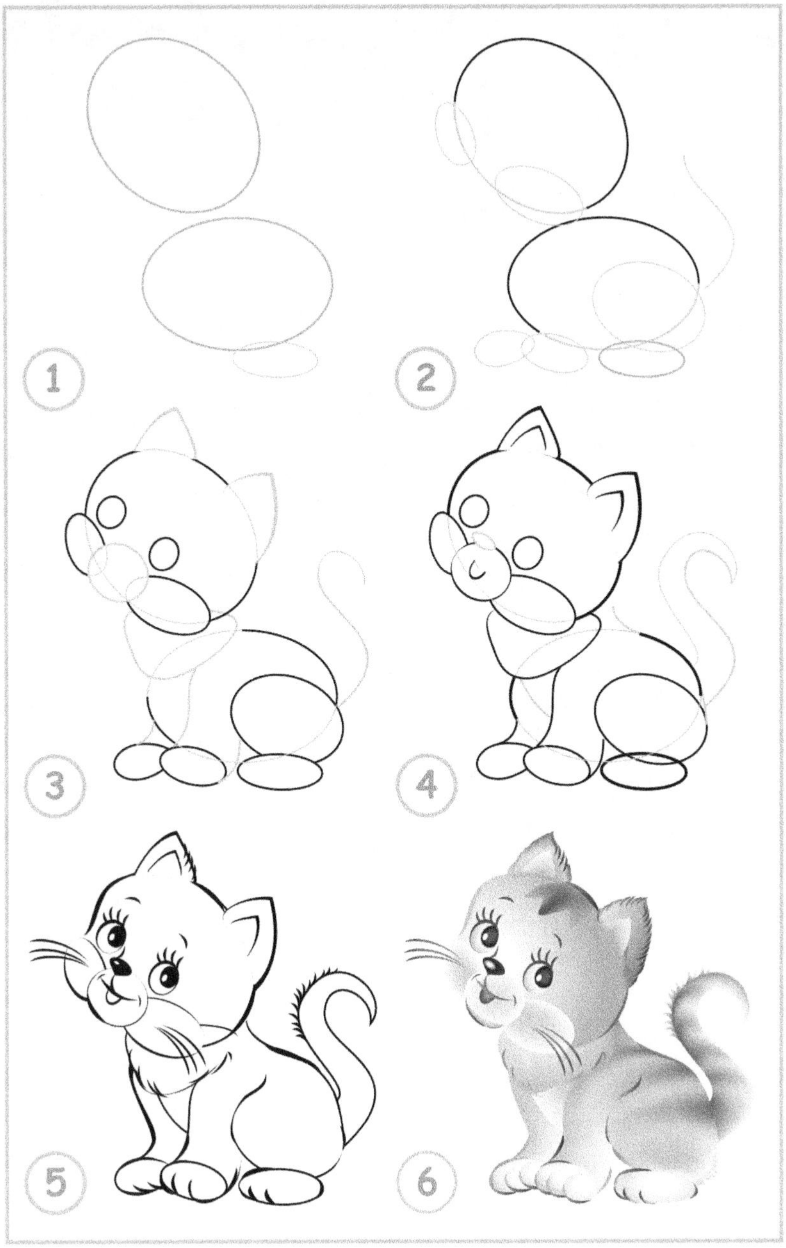
1
2
3
4
5
6

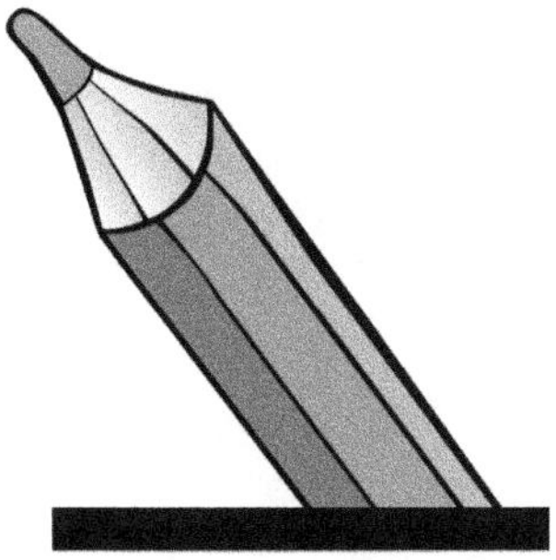

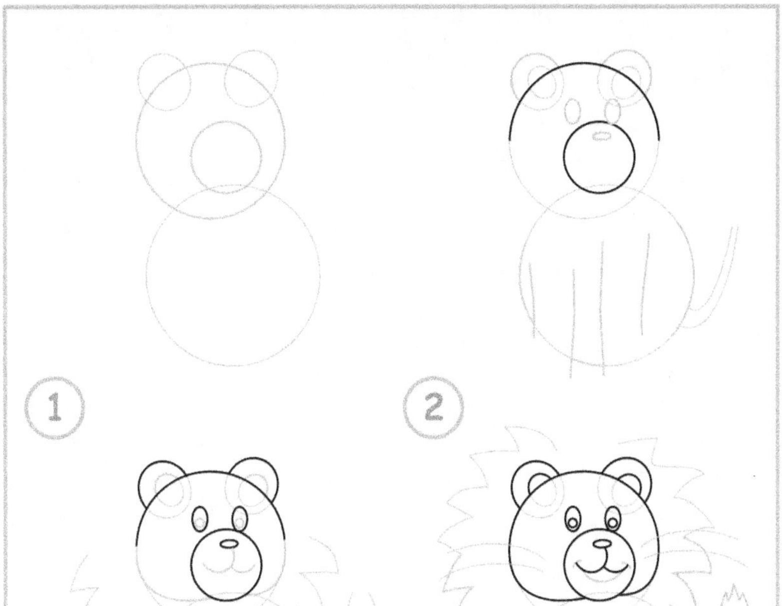
1
2
3
4
5
6

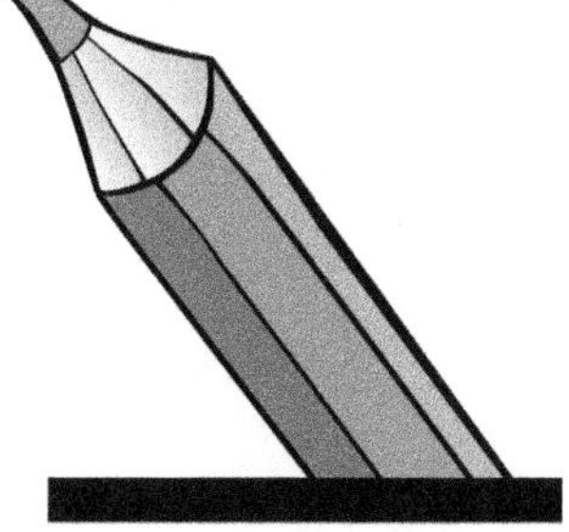

1
2
3
4
5
6

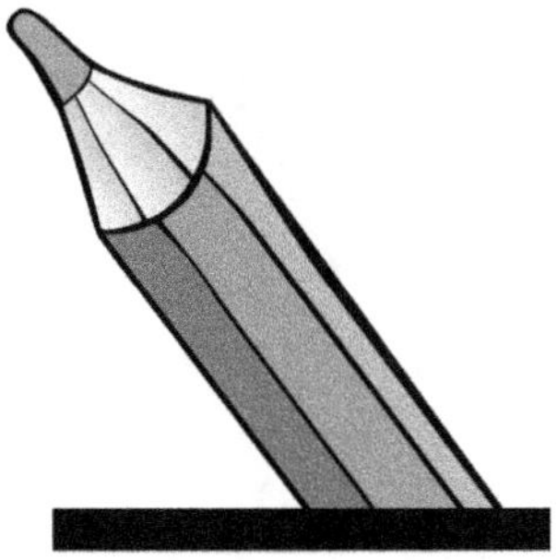

1
2
3
4
5
6

1
2
3
4
5
6

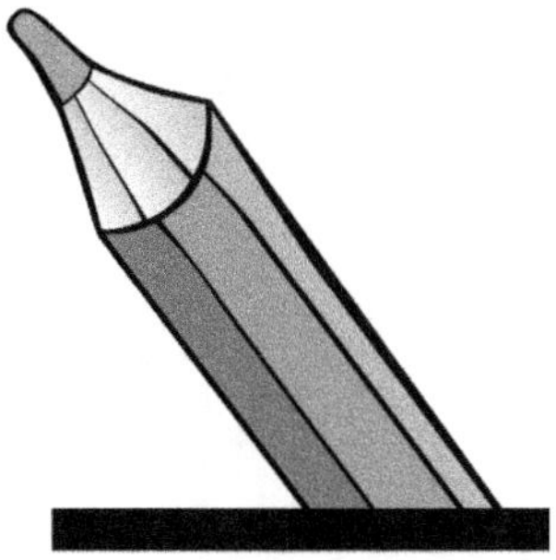

www.ingramcontent.com/pod-product-compliance
Lightning Source LLC
LaVergne TN
LVHW080249090426
835508LV00042BA/1511